YOUR KNOWLEDGE HAS VALUE

- We will publish your bachelor's and master's thesis, essays and papers

- Your own eBook and book - sold worldwide in all relevant shops

- Earn money with each sale

Upload your text at www.GRIN.com and publish for free

Bibliographic information published by the German National Library:

The German National Library lists this publication in the National Bibliography; detailed bibliographic data are available on the Internet at http://dnb.dnb.de .

This book is copyright material and must not be copied, reproduced, transferred, distributed, leased, licensed or publicly performed or used in any way except as specifically permitted in writing by the publishers, as allowed under the terms and conditions under which it was purchased or as strictly permitted by applicable copyright law. Any unauthorized distribution or use of this text may be a direct infringement of the author s and publisher s rights and those responsible may be liable in law accordingly.

Imprint:

Copyright © 2017 GRIN Verlag
Print and binding: Books on Demand GmbH, Norderstedt Germany
ISBN: 9783668725843

This book at GRIN:

https://www.grin.com/document/428702

Fanny S Alam

Hoax as A Threat Towards Nation's Diversity. A Challenge for Indonesian Government to Overcome It

A Case Study of Hoax Dissemination About Tanjung Balai in 2016

GRIN Verlag

GRIN - Your knowledge has value

Since its foundation in 1998, GRIN has specialized in publishing academic texts by students, college teachers and other academics as e-book and printed book. The website www.grin.com is an ideal platform for presenting term papers, final papers, scientific essays, dissertations and specialist books.

Visit us on the internet:

http://www.grin.com/

http://www.facebook.com/grincom

http://www.twitter.com/grin_com

Hoax as A Threat Towards Nation's Diversity:

A Challenge for Indonesian Government to Overcome It

(A Case Study of Hoax Dissemination About Tanjung Balai in 2016)

By Fanny S Alam

Abstract

Popularity of any type of media might be accomplished by various means, one of which is to disseminate hoax. As hoax is considered interesting or sensational with a purpose to attract attention or to enhance profit, media industry is always trapped to publish hoax since it is considered "a false truth". Particularly, social media has a huge tendency to disseminate hoax due to its speed capacity and flexibility to be accessed by public in various social , economy , and education statuses.

Apart of the purpose to attract attention or to enhance profit, hoax currently has become a sharp weapon to attack peace situation in the nation diversity. Indonesia with a very diverse circumstance is a priority target for hoax dissemination, principally the one regarding religion and political issues. Case of Tanjung Balai is one of the most dangerous hoaxes due to its negative impacts for the region and its local society. In national scale, it encourages negativity to minority groups, in this case Chinese and Non Moslems. Fortunately, local and national government anticipated it well and conducted strict enforce to the disseminating actor.

Through direct observation to various media and literature study, this paper is intended to uncover the threat of hoax for nation's diversity and how the government's attempt is to implement anticipating actions to eradicate further negative effects due to hoax dissemination in this country generally.

Keywords : Hoax, Nation's Diversity, Government's attempt

Introduction

It is inevitable to see numerous releases of media accessed by public openly. They have various interests and willingness while expecting public to be active through the use of media in voicing themselves. In here, media releases act as common carriers of conducting public discussion. They create a specific responsibility to form a basis for special privileges in terms of performing democratic society based on news and information received from any media provider.[1] At the same time, it is the task of journalism as its priority obligation to provide the truth.

Media are channels to work as a rich source of information. Most of information is processed so as to convey up to date news or even just to share any finding categorized bias in public. However, all media approve that they must conduct their work in accordance with truth as their basis. As mentioned by Bill Kovach in The Element of Journalism, truth in journalistic is a result coming from professional discipline in a regard of assembling and verifying facts. In the following time, it is relying on journalists' work to attempt to convey all the findings in such a fair and reliable way which can be subject to further investigation while possible.

Public are facing tremendous growth of media supported by the highlighted improvement of technology. Time gives evidence that media work can be enhanced through the technology development. It views almost no limitations for media to disseminate their work in any time any place. It is a borderless dissemination while allowing public to access any release with or no permission. Any access is available to maintain a space for public addressing their needs to criticize or just to share what across in their mind. Media create specific spaces to create free public interaction and are in line with the principle of democracy and openness.

One of the technology development impacts in media is the existence of social media. This type of media delivers various amazement, yet public realize that social media can be considered reliable while noticing their accessibility, prompt releases, and effortlessness to see previous releases. Flexibility is a word offered by social media because of their accessibility without borders of time and places.

Particularly, social media provide more spaces for public in active interactions in a correspondence of any issue released. Direct comments and responses can be illustrated as a part of democratic society in terms of sharing ideas and developing critical thinking. Broad range of issues in social media brings another new impact, that is the emergence of hoax effortlessly. Furthermore, leading media industry is sometimes connected to the release of hoax due to earning more profits and gaining popularity.

It is a great possibility to see hoax which might direct the way of public's thought

---

[1] Dean, Walter and Rosentiel, Tom, American Press Institute

openly. Despite its task to keep conveying the truth, media industry sometimes cannot avoid the hoax release. In fact, it shows a potent harm in deliberating public opinion with a potential to segregate public and nation's unity in a larger scale. Indonesia is the country with the most numerous access to social media, particularly Twitter and Facebook. This condition enables all participating online media to convey hoax with no difficulties for any purpose. However, hoax initiates some problems, one of which is regarding issues of diversity. One of hoaxes in Indonesia which used to encourage riot and segregation among public both regionally and nationally is the one in Tanjung Balai. At that time there was a case of a local woman mentioning her objection due to the voice of prayer call for Moslems considered distracting because it was considered too loud through the loudspeaker face to face directing to her house. Despite the well-conducted negotiation among the woman, local police, and seniors of the mosque, many people both local and national regions received the WhatsApp message saying that a prohibition of prayer call was suggested and requested all Moslems to stand for their rights in terms of this issue. More responses were revealed on Facebook and Twitter since the message was posted on both. In Tanjung Balai, the case triggered local people to act violating the law by burning Buddha temples and destroying most Chinese's properties. It withdrew the attention generally, particularly President of Republic of Indonesia, Joko Widodo, to request local and national apparatus to cooperate addressing the issue. A strict enforcement was performed by the police when managing to arrest the leading actor behind the hoax.

Through an intense observation of media news and literature study, this paper has a purpose to reveal how hoax might threaten diversity and nation's unity and how the government perform their attempt to overcome it. Role of the government is still considered significant to finally maintain conducive circumstance along with the willingness of public and media industry in creating more positive attitudes and elaborating facts and data to convey news and other types of information in public.

Discussion

Media and hoax are certainly inseparable. Hoax requires media to release its contents, therefore, it can be accessed by public openly. The dissemination of hoax is becoming broader due to the development of technology which supports any existing media industry. As stated by Paul Steiger, a Wall Street Journal Managing Editor that the ability to disseminate convincing lies is now more available.[2]

What it means by convincing lies is hoax. In media terminology, hoax, particularly media hoax, is described as a purposefully false story or account that is presented by a news organization as true. [3] Once hoax is disseminated, it provides public with

---

[2] Steiger, Paul, Wall Street Journal Managing Editor, Stanford Report, May 22, 2002

[3] Boyle, Patrick, The Hoax Project, Phillip Merril College of Journalism, University of Maryland, 2005

profoundly convincing information. It must be very influential as well due to the reality that public are easily encouraged emotionally better than thinking carefully and critically for what they are reading. The power of hoax is so succinct that it is able to make public justify one occurrence even without overviewing both accuracy and inaccuracy behind all the information. As said above mentioned in the introduction, hoax triggers public to act violating the law and this situation is supposed to be a specific concern for government and public as well.

Media hold the substantial role in disseminating hoax. In addition, the existence of particular media types, such as social media, penetrates hoax as truthfully accepted information as an account for being published even by some leading media. Lisa Clark, an expert in social media, reveals that hoax on social media is published like a chain mail. It is published in the proper rapidity, making public directed to push the button of share or retweet when discovering things which attract them[4]. Despite being proven inaccurate, most hoaxes on various media are in extensive demand to be published. It is unfortunate that public with willingness to convey hoax are considered to make a difference or merely to win some attractions.

Furthermore, ideally media act as a guardian profoundly to see information regarding social and government issues, because public believe they should be informed about both issues accurately. However, media are always encouraged to expose sensational issues, hoax or not, to attract more attention and to generate more profits. With these reasons, media are a means of dispersing information while they can possibly be manipulative.[5]

Hoax definitely outlaws the principle of journalistic truth which is supposed to promote fairness and reliability despite giving the space for public in disseminating their personal opinions responding hoax published on any media. Positively, it promotes public opinion creation while at the same time investigating the accuracy of it. Unfortunately, hoax is able to be used as a political and religion issue to contra with the peace circumstance in diversity. Particularly, it is what has been exposed in Indonesia as a diverse country. Hoax is conveyed openly through social media specifically to influence public opinion directed to particular political or religion group's intentions. Likewise, peace circumstance is in a critical situation to face segregations of public opinion which might lead to the nation's unity separation.

Diversity issues are always thought to have high level of sensitivity despite its significance to be introduced to diverse public in Indonesia. Furthermore, numerous hoaxes in regard to the issues in Indonesia have been escalating dramatically due to some factors, such as an influence to public in general election and a discredit to specific ethnics and religions. One of diversity issues used to escalate in social media dominantly, Tanjung Balai case in 2016. It emerged from a woman's objection to the

---

[4] Clark, Lisa, Social Media Rumors and Hoaxes, www.socialmediasun.com, 27 April 2012

[5] Grabber A, Doris, and Dunaway, Johanna, Mass Media and American Politics, CQ Sage, 2015

sound of prayer call from one mosque through a loudspeaker and it directed to her house. The protest was responded by inviting the local officials, police, and seniors of the mosque and everything was ended well as it had met a solution. However, an unexpected situation occurred when a WhatsApp message was conveyed massively, informing the prohibition of prayer call around the area of the mosque. Obviously, it promoted negativity and rage from most public, particularly from the ones who did not recognize the truth about the case previously. The case became a national headline due to the riot and some destructive actions to numerous properties belonging to Chinese ethnic society and the burning of some Buddha temples to add the worst. This situation was another new challenge of harmony in diversity between the majority (Islam groups) and minority (Buddhist, Chinese ethnic group). In addition, the message (later erased) became viral on social media, specifically Facebook and Twitter. Various responses appeared to share public opinion. The message managed to segregate public with positive and negative responses as a reaction to the emerging case at that time. It was unfortunate that most of negative reactions had an immense tendency to promote hatred and discrimination to a specific ethnic group.

It was very shocking noticing that the actor behind the message was not even a local of Tanjung Balai, yet he lived in Jakarta. He was arrested by the police after there was a release that the President of Republic of Indonesia, Joko Widodo, commanded a serious investigation through the case in order to avoid more escalating occurrences. Most of the messages contain hatred and provoking statements leading to the segregation of unity in public. For this reason, the actor was charged by Act 28 verse 2 junct Act 45 verse 2 and or Act 27 verse 3 junct verse 1 Law no 11 / 2008 about Electronic Technology Information and or Act 156 and or Act 160 Crime Act Law with maximum 6 year imprisonment.[6]

As a further feedback after the case, one of efforts of the government is to support any positive attempt to avoid hoax published on media. One workshop, titled " How to identify fake news and conduct content verification" was supported by the government, with the concern of inviting press and journalists in Council of Press in joint with Google and Editors Forum in a purpose to create media as curators or gate keepers to verify hoax instead of being hoax facilitators. It was said by Rudiantara, Minister of Communication Affairs that the government's attempt to handle developing contents was not focusing to conduct blocking any longer, but encouraging literacy, socialization, and education without any purpose to intervene organizations and communities. [7]

---

[6] http://megapolitan.kompas.com/read/2016/08/02/15510071/penyebar.ujaran.kebencian.terkait.kerusuhan.tanjungbalai.di.facebook.ditangkap.di.jagakarsa

[7] https://newswire.id/content/pemerintah-apresiasi-upaya-cegah-dan-berantas-hoax

Conclusion and Recommendation

It must be one of special awareness when discussing hoax and media since both of them are in pairs and with specific intentions, hoax is disseminated to reach the target of audiences of media planned previously. Hoax does not appear instantly, it is so properly planned that it resembles the truth and planned to be well accepted by various segments of public.

When considered inseparable with media, it does not mean hoax becomes a source of information for every media significantly. Aware or not, the existence of hoax is believed to enhance public attention and to generate income more for media. Despite violating principle of journalism, hoax is always on the top of release, with no exceptions for leading media industries. Hoax usually emerges in sensational titles while being manipulative, particularly for public who rarely recognize the accuracy and inaccuracy of any publication as well. This condition is used by media through their journalists to keep publishing hoax.

For more serious circumstance, hoax is a comprehensive threat which harms peace and harmony. In Indonesia, while the situation of diversity and harmony among various groups of ethnic and religion remains in peace, it can possibly be distracted by the emergence of hoax which has a specific purpose to provoke hatred and discredit to some ethnic and religion groups. It creates a wide segregation among public, as a consequence, in the future it breaks the harmony in unity as well. It can be overviewed through various responses revealed from social media. Positive and negative responses from hoax with sources of diversity issues have a serious tendency to segregate public which will terminate harmony in diversity.

It is recognized that media has the most significant role in disseminating fairness and truth plus objectivity as well for public. Media are responsible of releasing their publication as a part of literacy for public. In indirect ways, media must be educational, as a consequence they will be always having responsible contents to be conveyed to public. As one function of media is as a means of processing every information with fact verification and investigation if required, they must be capable of filtering negative information, one of which is hoax. Considered as truth, hoax is a part of convincing lies which furthermore can lead public to be in their negative overview when observing news or information and responding negatively with possible tendency of discrimination and discredit, specifically to minority and other different groups.

As a part of solutions, principally in Indonesia, the government used to act strictly to ban problematic websites with specific concern to provoke public in discriminating and intolerant practices. For current periods, the government has more elaborating attempts to conduct more literacy and education for public and media in terms of blocking fake information and hoax dissemination. It is considered as a sustainable long term work noticing that it requires thorough comprehension among media actors. In addition, it is imperative that the government and media actors lead public corresponding the fake news and hoax dissemination. Consequently, it leads public to convey and to see whether any information is both accurate and inaccurate. Eventually, to stop fake news and hoax dissemination is obviously a work of government, media, and public altogether, especially to maintain harmony in diversity of our country.

References:

1. Dean, Walter and Rosentiel, Tom, American Press Institute, www.americanpressinstitute.com
2. Kovach, Bill and Rosentiel, Tom, American Press Institute, www.americanpressinstitute.com
3. Steiger, Paul, Wall Street Journal Managing Editor, Stanford Report, May 22, 2002
4. Boyle, Patrick, The Hoax Project, Phillip Merril College of Journalism, University of Maryland, 2005
5. Clark, Lisa, Social Media Rumors and Hoaxes, www.socialmediasun.com, 27 April 2012
6. Grabber A, Doris, and Dunaway, Johanna, Mass Media and American Politics, CQ Sage, 2015
7. http://megapolitan.kompas.com/read/2016/08/02/15510071/penyebar.ujaran.kebencian.terkait.kerusuhan.tanjungbalai.di.facebook.ditangkap.di.jagakarsa
8. https://newswireid/content/pemerintah-apresiasi-upaya-cegah-dan-berantas-hoax

YOUR KNOWLEDGE HAS VALUE

- We will publish your bachelor's and master's thesis, essays and papers

- Your own eBook and book - sold worldwide in all relevant shops

- Earn money with each sale

Upload your text at www.GRIN.com and publish for free